February

Months of the Year

by Mari Kesselring
Illustrated by Paige Billin-Frye

Content Consultant:
Susan Kesselring, MA
Literacy Educator and Preschool Director

magic wagon

visit us at www.abdopublishing.com

Published by Magic Wagon, a division of the ABDO Group, 8000 West 78th Street, Edina, Minnesota 55439. Copyright © 2010 by Abdo Consulting Group, Inc. International copyrights reserved in all countries. All rights reserved. No part of this book may be reproduced in any form without written permission from the publisher.

Looking Glass Library™ is a trademark and logo of Magic Wagon.

Printed in the United States.

 PRINTED ON RECYCLED PAPER

Text by Mari Kesselring
Illustrations by Paige Billin-Frye
Edited by Patricia Stockland
Interior layout and design by Emily Love
Cover design by Emily Love

Library of Congress Cataloging-in-Publication Data
Kesselring, Mari.
 February / by Mari Kesselring ; illustrated by Paige Billin-Frye ; content consultant, Susan Kesselring.
    p. cm. — (Months of the year)
 ISBN 978-1-60270-629-3
 1. February—Juvenile literature. 2. Calendar—Juvenile literature. I. Billin-Frye, Paige, ill. II. Kesselring, Susan. III. Title.
 CE13.K4725 2010
 398'.33—dc22
                              2008050693

January is the month
that starts a whole year.
What is the next month?
Say it loud so I'll hear.

Did you say February?
That's good. Hooray!
This short, wintery month
has just 28 days.

But every four years
it has day 29.
Then it's called leap year.
Won't that be fine?

February is always
month number two.
Think of the many things
that you want to do.

floss

toothpaste

February is for dental health.
Keep your mouth clean.
Brush your teeth often
and check in between!

February's still winter.

It can have lots of snow.

Sledding, skiing, and skating—

just look at you go!

Do you know how long
the winter will stay?
Find out on day two—
it's Groundhog Day.

14

On Valentine's Day,
we think of people we love.
We make cards for our friends.
Draw a heart and a dove!

George Washington

Abraham Lincoln

18

One Monday this month
is Presidents' Day.
We wish George and Abe
a happy birthday!

19

It is Black History Month
all month long.
We learn about leaders
and sing them a song!

Oh my, what a short month!

February is over.

March is the next month.

Time to find four-leaf clovers!

MARCH

23

Valentine's Day Cookies

Have an adult help you make sugar cookies for Valentine's Day. Find a cookie cutter in the shape of a heart and decorate the baked cookies with frosting. Then, give them to your friends for Valentine's Day!

Shadow or No Shadow?

Do you think the groundhog will see its shadow this February? Write down your guess! On February 2, check the news to find out if the groundhog saw its shadow. Did you guess right?

Words to Know

clover—a small, green plant.
January—the first month of the year. It comes after December.
leap year—when the year has 366 days instead of 365.
March—the third month of the year. It comes after February.

Web Sites

To learn more about February, visit ABDO Group online at **www.abdopublishing.com**. Web sites about February are featured on our Book Links page. These links are routinely monitored and updated to provide the most current information available.